ONE TRUTH THAT CHANGES EVERYTHING

THANK YOU, BROOKE.

Rich

ALSO BY RILEY K. SMITH

How to Be a Couple and Still Be Free
with co-author Tina B. Tessina, Ph.D.

True Partners:
A Workbook for Building
a Lasting Intimate Relationship
with co-author Tina B. Tessina, Ph.D.

One Truth that Changes Everything

Riley K. Smith, MA, LMFT

PRECOCITY PRESS

One Truth That Changes Everything is a work of nonfiction. Except for my history, names and case history details have been changed. *RKS*

Editorial Guidance: Brooke Warner and Ira Rifkin
Copy editor: Susan Peters
Design & Illustrations: Riley K. Smith
Cover Art: Rockwell Kent
Creative Director: Susan Shankin
Author photo: Monty Rowan

ISBN: 978-0-9987963-4-5

Published by Precocity Press
612 Santa Clara Avenue, Venice, CA 90291
www.precocitypress.com

First edition. Printed and bound in the United States of America

CONTENTS

Prologue vii

Preface ix

To Begin xi

1. The Premise 13

2. The Origin of the Lie 17

3. How The Lie Affects Our Lives 25

4. The Truth 35

5. The Prime Directive 51

Appendix 63

Footnotes and Resources 73

About the Author 75

Prologue

WHY I WROTE "ONE TRUTH"

First, I wrote it for myself. I wrote it for myself because One Truth is, in many ways, my "prime directive" and I wanted to synthesize it and clarify it for myself. I also wrote it for myself because I am excited. I'm excited about the concept and the positive outcome of using it in my life and in passing it on to my clients for their use. I am also excited because, when I look at the human species—our interactions and our history—through this lens, things such as imperialism, genocide, racism, etc. that in the past have been incomprehensible to me begin to make sense. I am particularly excited because One Truth carries within it a path to resolve those painful, self-defeating aspects of Being Human.

Second, I wrote it for my clients and students. Although this particular way of understanding why people do what they do is not new to many in the field of psychotherapy, I personally had not seen it expressed succinctly in this way in plain language. Further, I became aware that my psychotherapy students and supervisees had not been immersed, even in their graduate degree courses, to this way of understanding and working with themselves and their clients.

Third, I wrote it in appreciation. Jack Lee Rosenberg, DDS, PhD, and Beverly Kitaen-Morse, PhD, husband and wife, were my mentors and teachers. Beginning in the mid-1970s Jack created Integrative Body Psychotherapy (IBP)[1] and Beverly collaborated with Jack, honed the concepts and implementation and managed the IBP training institute. I began my training in the late-1990s and by 2004, was privileged to teach therapists in the training program. IBP changed my life and my practice as a psychotherapist.

Most of this writing has its roots in IBP.

Thank you, Jack and Beverly, with all my heart.

Jack Lee Rosenberg passed away in November, 2015.

God Bless.

Preface

I'm a psychotherapist. As such I'm interested in root causes. I want to know and I want my clients to know how it makes sense that they are struggling—with anxiety, depression, addiction, relationships or whatever is troubling them. Although it isn't always obvious, ultimately it always makes sense. There is always a root and that's where the healing happens. The anxiety clears. The depression lifts. The addiction loosens its grip. The relationship regains its footing or the partners move on.

I've practiced for over 40 years. I've used and taught somatic psychotherapy for the last 20 years and I want to share with you what I've come to believe are the fundamental sources, the roots, of human strife and of human well-being. That belief is the basis of my own inner peace and my work as a psychotherapist. Hopefully you will be able to use these concepts, this cosmology, to further your own path to peace as a member of this mystifying, fractious and wonderful species we call Humankind.

Riley K. Smith, MA, LMFT

To Begin

This book is subjective. It's *my truth—my experience.* My inner skeptic is satisfied that what I say here is true. I've proved it to myself and I'll do my best to explain how. But I can't prove it to you or anyone else. Hopefully it will make sense to you and lead you to your own personal exploration and experiments.

Also implicit in this work is my conviction that our beliefs create our personal reality, not the other way around. Our primal view of ourselves and the world is set by the time we are somewhere around three years old or even earlier. From that time on our experiences are colored by that view—even to the point that experiences that don't fit our basic assumption are ignored or distorted in order to fit that view. I'll explain more fully in the section on Attachment Theory in Chapter Two.

Our beliefs create our reality

Also note that my observations and beliefs are not original. Most of what I write here is well established in the field of psychology. What may be original is my description of my personal process and my conclusion about Changing Everything.

So we begin.

One TRUTH that changes everything

CHAPTER I
the Premise

In the midst of personal upset and public upheaval, seeking peace of mind and heart, I have come to believe that almost everyone carries a deeply held lie that is the foundation of human suffering:

I AM FUNDAMENTALLY BAD,
UNLOVABLE AND/OR UNACCEPTABLE.

Living from that misunderstanding, keeps us in a constant, if unconscious, state of fear, shame and defensiveness. That lie drives aggression, hurt, betrayal, greed, hatred, lying, hunger for power and control, living as victims, depression, imperialism, competition and addiction.

Contrary to almost universal consensus, this is the truth, the truth that can set us free:

I AM EXQUISITELY WHO AND WHAT
I AM SUPPOSED TO BE. I AM, IN MY
CORE NATURE, LOVEABLE, WORTHY
AND GOOD. I AM A FINITE AND
PERSONAL EXPRESSION OF THE
INFINITE CONSCIOUSNESS.

When we REALLY, TRULY trust this to be true, we are free. We can breathe.

We can live our true selves, motivated not by fear or shame, but by inspiration, aspiration and love. When we live our lives from a certainty that we are perfectly okay, we stand at the doorway to infinite possibilities.

SO, EVERYTHING CHANGES

I know the change can be made. Many have done it. I've done it, over many years and imperfectly, but I have done it. I have seen my clients do it. I know that anyone, with the will and commitment, can do it.

This writing, then, is intended to explain how I came to believe that my premise is true. I offer it as an enticement, a proposal and an invitation to consider taking this path to inner peace and personal power in this age of upheaval and anxiety.

Your path is likely different from mine. You will have to find it for yourself. My hope is that by describing my path as best I can, you can awaken to the possibility and be inspired to find and follow your own path to peace and power.

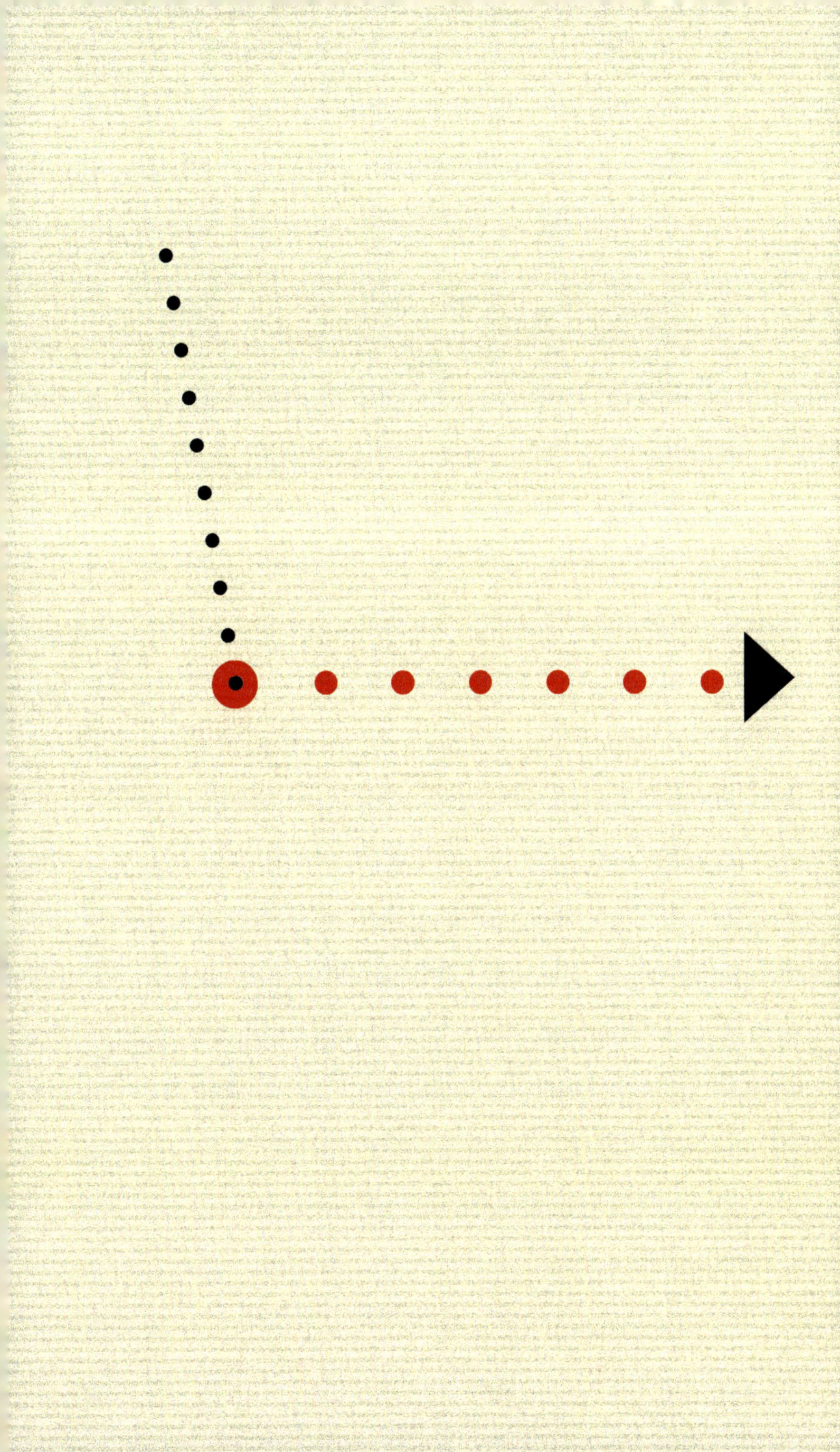

I AM not good enough.

i am ALONE.

i am unlovable.

I AM UNWORTHY.

ATTACHMENT THEORY

CHAPTER 2 the Origin of the Lie

Attachment theory[2] is a generally accepted psychological theory that posits that harmful or incomplete attachment experiences (including varying degrees of abuse and neglect) in infancy and through childhood lead us to experience and to assume that we are somehow flawed, i.e., "I'm not loveable, I'm not good enough or I'm unworthy." We carry this misunderstanding, mostly unawares and unchallenged, deep in our psyche, our body and in our primal memory. (I call it the Basic Wound[3].) We then proceed to develop a system of coping strategies in an effort to fix our wound, conceal the "fact" and/or protect ourselves from the pain of that belief. Further, that fundamental assumption serves as a filter, eliminating from our consciousness all evidence that it might not be true. For instance, to the extent that my early childhood experience leads me to assume that I'm not loveable, any love that comes to me is discounted. Unless I make a conscious effort to be aware of it, this process is automatic and unconscious.

IMPORTANT NOTE: DON'T BLAME YOUR MOTHER. In order to accept the premise that our upset derives from unmet attachment needs, I found that it was helpful to understand that *attachment injuries have been passed down from generation to generation for eons.* Our parents, our grandparents and their parents before them had attachment wounds and as a result they couldn't give their children what they hadn't received. Very few parents aren't doing the best they know how.

THE BASIC WOUND

RILEY'S STORY. Through introspection, intuition, logic, flashbacks and family stories I've assembled from my own psychotherapy, I have been able to put together a narrative of my preverbal attachment experience and here is a part of what I believe happened:

I was lucky to have a couple of nice people for parents. They were excited to be parents and I was their first. Now, their impediment was that they both had lost parents in their childhood. I came along and they didn't trust that they knew how to parent an infant. So, they bought a book on child-care. In the mid-nineteen thirties, the conventional wisdom on child-care said, once you put your baby down at night, let him cry or you'll spoil him.

So, my first crisis, my first attachment injury, was being alone in the dark, in my crib, at a developmental stage where I needed instant Mom. I needed loving attunement, skin to skin, on demand.

So, as a tiny infant, my experience every night was that I was alone, calling for attention, and nothing happened. I was upset — scared, lonely, abandoned, angry, and/or frustrated—and nothing I did made anything happen. My experience was, "I am all alone and nothing I say or do solves my problem." That experience led me to a false assumption about myself that I am essentially unimportant, unlovable, unworthy and incompetent. *That primal misunderstanding is the root of my sense of shame about myself. It is my* Basic Wound.

SOFIA'S STORY. Sofia's conception was an inconvenient accident, a result of her mom's lapse in thoughtful self-care. Her mom and her dad were a little buzzed when they met at a party. She took him home that night. They had a great time. About a month later Sofia had made her impending presence known and her father was long gone.

Sofia gestated in the powerful mix of her mom's anguish and indecision about whether to abort or not, the prospect of single motherhood, a dramatic shift in lifestyle and determination to do the right thing. Out of a strong sense of personal integrity and growing love for the child-to-be in her womb, Sofia's mom committed herself to motherhood and to making the best life she could for herself and her child. It wasn't easy. Sofia was loved, but from infancy she spent a lot of time in childcare and her mom was usually tired and only partially available after work. There were also good times on and off with Sofia's grandparents who adored her.

Against the background of the love of her mother and grandparents, much of Sofia's experience from infancy was that of being fatherless, the source of her mother's anxiety, and a burden and that her need for consistent, loving connection was unmet. That experience led her to believe that she was unworthy and undesirable and is the essence of her Basic Wound.

ALONSO'S STORY. Alonso's mom had lousy taste in men (probably because his mom's father was an angry man). Alonso's dad was mean when he was drunk and he was often drunk. He abused his wife and his son. Alonso and his mom were afraid of him and his mom couldn't protect Alonso.

Alonso grew up afraid. He lived in the aura of his mom's fear as well as his own fear of his father. His experience of being the object of his father's disapproval and unprotected by his mother left him anxious and certain that he was bad and unworthy—his Basic Wound.

ABBIE'S STORY. Abbie's dad was a good man who worked hard and earned enough to make ends meet. Her mom loved kids and did some child care to supplement the family income. Her parents were solid people who loved their kids. Abbie was the fourth child with two more to follow. Her attachment challenge was mainly twofold. First there just wasn't enough of mom (or dad) to go around. Abbie's older sister helped care for the siblings, but there is only so much parenting a child can do. Second, with six children competing for nurture and support, there was not only a shortage, but there was constant chaos and no personal space. Abbie was lost in the middle. Abbie's Basic Wound was her experience of not enough nurture and too much confusion and conflict leading her to believe that she was unimportant, undeserving and under siege.

i'M

good

enough

COPING STRATEGY

In the field of psychology there are several terms for Coping Strategies. They are called Defenses, Neuroses, Addictions, Complexes, and Disorders to name a few. I call them Coping Strategies because I consider that to be the most generally accurate description and because it implies the root cause, the primal misunderstanding caused by attachment and developmental needs not met, the Basic Wound. Coping Strategies are a complex pattern of fixed muscular holding, energy blocks, emotional responses, and behaviors as well as beliefs about the self and the world. We develop these strategies in order to survive and thrive in our family environment. Coping Strategies are not pathology. They are normal. Everyone has Coping Strategies because no one gets out of childhood unscathed.

Although they were necessary for getting along when we were children, *Coping Strategies become problematic because they survive in our response to life's stresses as adults*. To the extent that

no one • • • • • • gets out • • • • • • of childhood • • • • • • unscathed we conduct our lives from these strategies they limit our ability to thrive and are the cause of stress, ill health and unhappiness.

I think of the complex pattern of Coping Strategies as a pseudo-personality. I picture it as a thick shell around our core selves because it covers, protects and suppresses who we really are. When we are living our Coping Strategies, we have little or no awareness of our true selves.

AUTOMATIC & UNCONSCIOUS

We are more or less in emergency defensive mode and *it's automatic and unconscious.* Coping Strategies limit our ability to be alive, here and now. They limit our ability to be intimate and vulnerable. They limit our ability to express our true selves and live passionately. Some typical Coping Strategies are addictions, spacing out, numbing, defensiveness, aggression, neglecting self to take care of or accommodate others, isolating, obsessing and phobias.

RILEY'S STORY. As an adult, when something happened that I experienced as similar to my original stressful situation, my Basic Wound would be activated and my Coping Strategies would kick in.

Here's one example of how a Coping Strategy played out. In college, defending, in part, against my shame and belief that I was unlovable and not good enough, I was socially and politically active (Coping Strategy). One of the most attractive young women on campus let it be known that she was interested in me. I was so convinced that I was unlovable that at the end of our first date, as I took her home, I explained to her that I knew that she was only interested in me because I was prominent on campus. She was so hurt that she never spoke to me again. It was years later that I finally understood what I had done and why.

That's one example of my personal version of a Coping Strategy. Your Coping Strategies are likely different. There are infinite variations, but they all are built on the lie and, if you know what to look for, you'll recognize your Basic Wound and understand how your Coping Strategies makes sense.

LOUIS' STORY. Louis was the fourth child born to a "trophy wife" mom who was overwhelmed with life and not available to her kids, and a very successful investment banker dad who was distant, judgmental and a harsh disciplinarian. Louis grew up in luxury. He and his siblings were cared for by a series of nannies. Louis' nurturing needs were only occasionally met and he was regularly and harshly reminded that he did not meet his father's expectations (Attachment Injuries).

He learned to assume that he had to live without love, appreciation and value. Based on this early experience, he mistakenly assumed that he was unlovable, incompetent and unacceptable. From those basic assumptions about himself, from that place of shame (his Basic Wound), he set out to cope as best he could. Building on this deeply held misunderstanding he grew up to be closed-hearted, jealous, acquisitive, judgmental, sensitive to criticism, constantly cheating, and striving for money and success in business (Coping Strategies).

ELIZABETH'S STORY. Elizabeth's mom was depressed. She hoped that having a baby would cheer her up and give her a purpose. So, Elizabeth was conceived to fix her mother. Because she was depressed, her mom couldn't give baby Elizabeth enough of the unconditional love and nurturing that she needed (Attachment Injury). In addition, Elizabeth experienced her mom's disappointment that "the baby" didn't make her feel better. That led Elizabeth to the assumption that she was unlovable and incompetent (Basic Wound). She believed that her purpose in life was to take care of people so they would value her even though she wasn't good enough. She learned to focus on the needs of others and neglect her own needs and aspirations (Coping Strategy). As an adult Elizabeth was a social worker in a non-profit community center and was depressed.

EVERYONE HAS A STORY. Studies have shown that a majority of violent offenders in prison were severely traumatized as small children through serious neglect and/or violent abuse. Sometimes high-performing athletes are driven to win in order to prove their worth from a deeply held certainty that they aren't good enough. Very wealthy people sometimes can't acquire enough to assuage their conviction that they aren't good enough. People growing up in poverty sometimes live life from a conviction that they are powerless and unworthy. People sometimes cope with the conviction that they are unlovable by settling for the pseudo-love of sexual promiscuity.

Sometimes when parents are harsh and punitive a child will give up on being loved and close his or her heart. This seems to be more noticeable with boys who are expected to be tough instead of tender or "weak." This Coping Strategy eliminates the choice of being vulnerable and compassionate, and put together with a feeling that "I'm not good enough," can account for bullying behavior.

People's Coping Strategies often lead them to their role in society. One common strategy is being reactive to perceived orders or obligations, to automatically say "no" and to be averse to following instructions. It is very often a defining influence in being late, cutting classes, collecting parking tickets or living as an outlaw. This Coping Strategy led me to choose self-employment over a corporate career. I've been happily self-employed since 1972.

ABBIE'S STORY. Out of Abbie's sense that she was unworthy and undesirable (Basic Wound), she became a "caretaker" in order to feel valued (Coping Strategy). She discovered that she could do well in school and that school, unlike the chaos of her family, was a stable place where she could belong. She made it her home. Her Coping Strategy led her to become a much appreciated and successful grade school teacher.

PLEASE NOTE

I have used "sometimes" and "often" as a qualifier when I give examples of how Coping Strategies can influence our lives. That's because none of these outcomes are inevitable or predictable. Difficulties in childhood can both inspire *and* wound. The difficulties can crush us, they can inspire us and they can set us on our path. Sometimes the path is to heal ourselves, sometimes the path is one of service to ourselves and others. More often it is both. The process by which a person goes one way or the other is a mystery to me. Meanwhile, as I have said, I am a psychotherapist and as such, my job is to help people who are currently focused on a path of self-healing. The people who come to me are experiencing the troubling aspects of their Coping Strategies. This book is mainly for them.

So what happens when we realize that we've built at least part of our life on a huge misunderstanding?

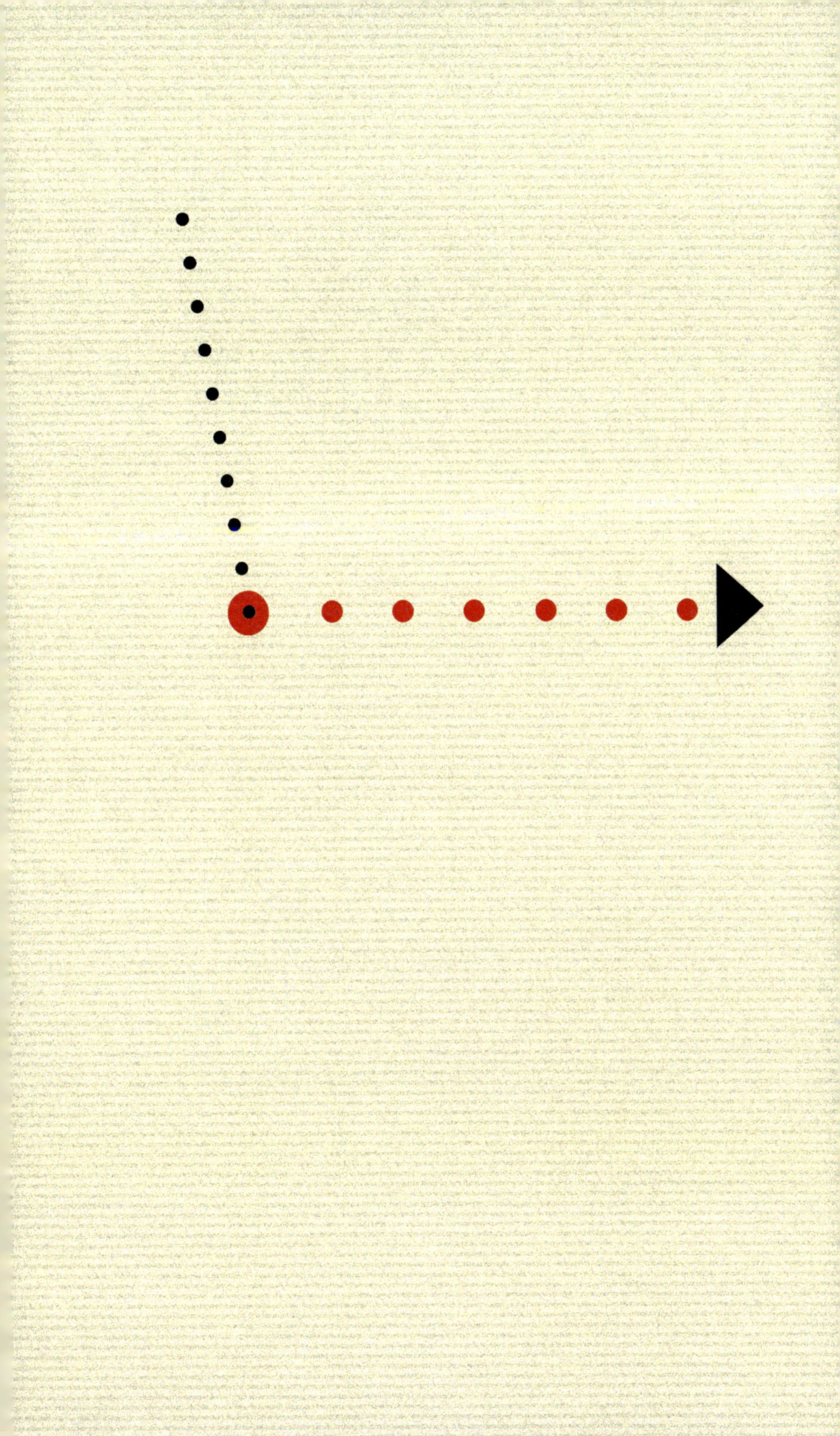

that

sets

us

NOW FOR THE GOOD NEWS

The Basic Wound is a mistake, a lie, a tragic misunderstanding. The truth is that every one of us is *essentially* good, lovable, worthy and exactly who we are supposed to be—always were and always will be. Our natural, inborn self is innocent, loving, lovable, worthy, energetic, optimistic, inspired, assertive and expressive.

HOW DO I KNOW?

Sorry, I can't prove objectively or scientifically that we are all lovable, worthy and exactly who we are supposed to be. I know it experientially, anecdotally and intuitively and I'll explain as best I can.

I LIVE IT

I've lived from shame and the assumption that I'm not lovable and I know that the result of that experience is that I was unable to sustain an intimate relationship. I was depressed, self-protective, jealous, oppositional, anxious, and unkind. Once I was able, with effort and over time, to make a shift and begin to live from the certainty that I am lovable and exactly who I am supposed to be, everything changed. I became more compassionate, relational, optimistic, and generous. I am no longer depressed or anxious. I am calm and grounded and I can sustain that state even when there is chaos and upset around me. Disclaimer: This statement is approximately 90% true. There are times when the old program, the Basic Wound and subsequent Coping Strategies, are triggered. At those times, however, I understand what has happened and I breathe, remember the truth and return to my Core Self, calm and grounded.

I SEE OTHERS LIVE IT

I see some of my friends and colleagues living it. I have the privilege of witnessing my therapy clients learning to live the new truth just as I have.

BRYAN. Bryan was a good man who had mastered his vocation. He competed with others at his company and was the top man. He made plenty of money, had a satisfying marriage to a good and successful woman and he had a good dog. He strived. He took vacations. He had digestive problems and said his belly was too big. Bryan was motivated by the competitive challenge and the desire for more money.

And Bryan was angry a lot. He was mad at his wife and yelled at his dog and he didn't know why. That's what he'd come in to see me about.

Bryan had done his work well. He had identified his Basic Wound. He was firstborn. His little sister developed an inoperable brain tumor when she was a toddler and the family focus was on her needs. His parents were distraught. Bryan not only lost his share of the nurture and attention, but was enrolled in attending to his sister's needs at a very young age. His role and his value in the family became that of a caretaker and mentor for his beloved sister. At that young age Bryan saw himself as responsible for the well-being of his family. Then, when he was 10 years old, his sister died. Bryan had totally failed. Not only had he forgone his own nurturing needs in a failed effort to not burden his parents, but he couldn't save his beloved sister! He expressed his Basic Wound as, "I am not only unimportant but I'm incompetent as well." One of his leading Coping Strategies was to strive constantly to prove his worth, while having no hope of succeeding. No wonder he was mad.

Bryan was committed to his therapy. He was aware of his Basic Wound and how it came to be. He was aware that his constant striving was a Coping Strategy. He was learning to live his new truth, "I am not bad because I couldn't fix my family. I am important. I am competent. I am good enough. In fact, I am exactly who I am supposed to be."

i'm not bad because i couldn't fix my family

After seeing me for about a year, he came to a session and declared, "I'm not mad anymore. In fact I'm doing very well, but I'm dissatisfied, bored and exhausted. There must be something more."

I asked him "Why do you compete and aspire to more wealth?"

He reflected and responded, "Maybe I'm not good enough and I'm hoping I'll be good enough if I constantly win and have increasingly more money." (Basic Wound and Coping Strategy)

"What if you're already perfect?" I asked. "You've mastered The Game. You're the best at what you do. You've maximized your effort to be good enough and found it unconvincing. It may be time to BE, in peace, inspired and entitled to be comfortable. It may be time to PLAY the game–for fun. Imagine that you are exactly who you are supposed to be. Now imagine your life from there."

Bryan was good at imagining and I could see him considering the image. His gut relaxed with a great belch, the tension left his face, his striving disappeared and he declared, "I am exactly what and who I need to be. I'm part of the fabric of the universe."

LISA[4]. Lisa sat up on the table, beaming, and exclaimed, "I'm only human . . . and that's exactly enough!"

Six months before, Lisa who was in her mid-twenties, had come to me unhappy with her life. She was functioning well enough—living with a roommate, financially supported by her controlling father and passive, childlike mother and working to build a career as a graphic designer. She complained of being averse to relationships with men and didn't trust women. Talented, smart and attractive, Lisa felt inadequate, unlovable and ashamed.

During the time that I worked with Lisa, in conjunction with attachment insight work, body awareness and teaching her self-nurturing and self-support techniques, I had been teaching Lisa to build and hold a charged state in her body using a particular way of breathing that builds energy throughout the body. When the energy is contained instead of discharged it energizes, relaxes tension and creates a felt experience of total aliveness and presence.

Getting there, however, often required addressing somatic blocks and energetic "speed limits" at the psychological level.

A part of her complex family-of-origin dynamic was Lisa's role in the family as that of a little girl. As a result, there was nowhere in her internalized family system for her to feel or experience herself as the grown woman that she was. Physically, she had to deny her woman-ness. This became apparent when breathing while lying down. When she began to feel alive in her body, she could feel her breasts and pelvic area. Her first few experiences of this led her to "split off." She got dizzy and spacey and couldn't continue the charging breath.

I was able to guide her through this "block." First I asked her to make the connection to her family of origin. Once she understood her psychological (Coping Strategy) need to be the child, Lisa was able to discover the parental messages that were missing in order for her to grow up. The next step was to coach her in self-nurturing using what I call Good Parent Messages—the basic nurturing that all children need to thrive.[5]

The Good Parent Messages most useful to Lisa were: *I see you and I hear you. It is not what you do, but who you are that I love. I love you and I give you permission to be different from me. I'll take care of you. You can trust your inner voice. I am proud of you. I have confidence in you and I know you will succeed. I give you permission to love and enjoy your erotic sexuality with a partner of your choice and not lose me.*

it's not what you do but who you are that i love

I coached Lisa on how to build a charge in her body with the breathing. Then, from that place of well-being, to say and write the Good Parent Messages to herself while tracking the sensations in her body—sensations of warmth and relaxation. Having embodied the self-support and self-nurture she could now complete the breathing series without splitting off.

Lisa could celebrate the somatic experience of her woman self—her whole self. That was the point where Lisa sat up on the table and with great joy, said, "I'm only human!"

DAVID. "I haven't been able to sleep or think straight for two days," David was talking as he came through the door and sat down in the chair.

This was David's fourth session.[4] I had learned his history. I had helped him identify his Basic Wound. He had responded well when I introduced him to Charge Breathing leading to a feeling of aliveness and calm.

David slouched in the chair looking miserable. I asked him if he'd like to learn how to get himself out of "the miseries." He nodded and said he did, looking slightly hopeful. I guided him through a process I call Steps Out of Fragmentation.[6]

"First, notice that you are fragmented.[7] What you're experiencing right now and for the last two days, the upset you feel, we'll call it *fragmented*. Now describe it as best you can."

"I made a mistake at work and it came out in a meeting. I felt exposed and ashamed, just like when I was a kid at school."

"What's the feeling in your body?"

"My face is hot. My solar plexus is on fire. I want to cry but I can't breathe."

"Anything else?"

"My mind is racing. That's why I can't sleep."

"All those feelings and thoughts are parts of being fragmented. That's the experience of being fragmented."

Now, identify the fragmenting event or events, "When did you fragment? What was the last time you were calm?"

"I was calm when I went into the meeting. When my boss identified my mistake, I felt like I'd been pole-axed and I've been like this ever since."

"OK, now tell me what happened in your childhood that felt that way—the earlier the better."

He told of an experience of being shamed in class when he was in second grade, "I had been daydreaming and so I misunderstood the question the teacher asked. I thought I knew the answer and so I shouted it out without waiting to be called on. I totally got it wrong. The whole class laughed at me, including the teacher."

"What nurturing or parenting was missing in that moment that would have soothed or prevented the upset?"

As he speculated, I made a note of the missing nurturing messages: *I see you and I hear you. It's not what you do, but who you are that I love. I'll take care of you. If you make a mistake, I'll help you fix it. You don't have to be alone anymore.*

Then, I coached him in Charge Breathing until he was energized, present, alert and calm.

I then fed him the nurturing messages that he had identified, one at a time. He repeated them until he could experience the effect of each one as a body sensation. Each message deepened the relaxation and calm that he felt until he was peaceful and present.

Finally, I asked him, "Think about the upsetting event at work and tell me what you experience right now."

"I've lost the upset about it and it doesn't feel like a catastrophe anymore. It just seems to be a problem to solve."

I've got your back

CHARGE BREATHING[8]

I mentioned breathing as part of the work I was doing with Lisa and David. I will describe it in more detail in the appendix. For now I will only say that, as part of my training in Integrative Body psychotherapy, I was taught a way to breathe that takes me to a physical, emotional, mental and spiritual experience of profound well-being. It's an experience of Core Self or essential Self, where there is a felt sense of *"I am exactly right, I am OK, I am exquisitely worthy."*

As a daily practice over time it helped change everything for me. That experience of well-being became the prime directive of my existence. The breathing was significant to Bryan, Lisa, David and my own transformation. It continues to be a dependable tool for restoring my equanimity.

LITTLE KIDS

Another proof, totally subjective and experiential, that we are essentially lovable and good is the experience I have of being with a toddler. It is impossible for me not to see the sweetness and innocence there.

I made a new friend at the market recently. She's about three years old. She was with her mom and she had a half grown puppy on a leash and a great big smile. As I walked past her she spoke up, "I have new dog and his name is Tony!" She was practically vibrating with joy. Enchanted, I stopped to chat and maybe to bask in her excitement, "Well, hello Tony. Can I pet him?" "Yes. He's a very good dog and Mom let him sleep with me last night!" We chatted briefly and went on about our day. I carried the warmth of that encounter for the rest of the day.

I can have a similar experience when I look at photos of myself as a young child. I have a photo of me sitting at a tiny table about to blow out the two candles on my birthday cake. Sweet. There have been times when I've been caught in the shame of my Basic Wound when I would do some breathing, get out that photo and remember the truth. It almost always helps.

WHAT IF IT'S NOT TRUE THAT I'M REALLY OK?

What if I'm wrong? What if I'm living in an ice-cream-and-cotton-candy fantasy that I made up because the truth is unbearable?

the Truth is in the Doing

I lived my early life from the assumption that I wasn't good enough. I lived from shame and I didn't like it very much. In the last 20 years or so, I've come to live my life assuming that I AM good enough. I like it a lot better. My family and friends like me better, too. The bottom line is, even if I really am a worthless loser, I much prefer the results I'm getting by choosing to live as if I am essentially good and lovable. When I changed my prime directive, the quality of my life seriously improved.

For me, the truth is in the doing.

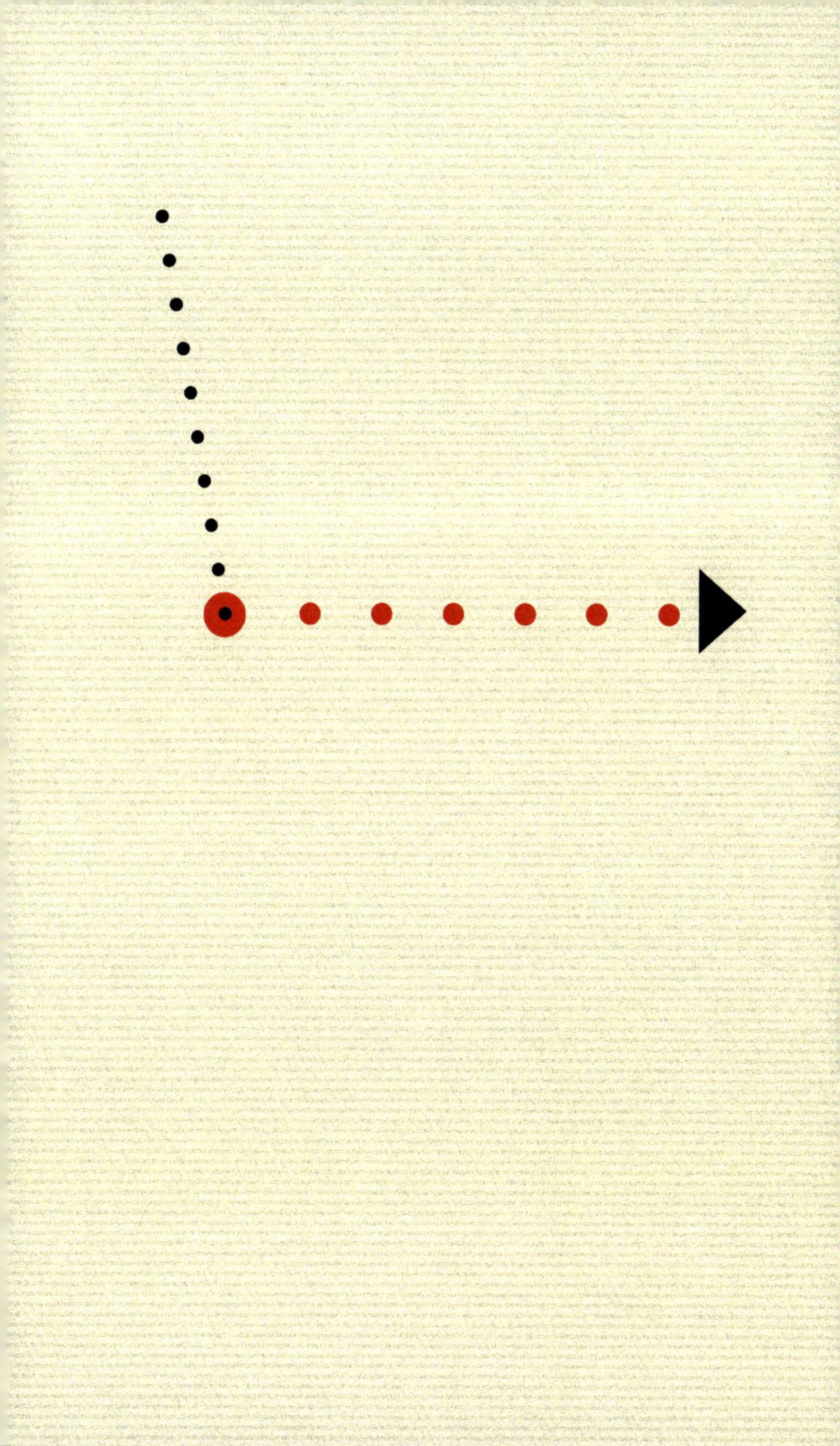

Exchanging THE old LIE for the new **** truth.

CHAPTER 5
the Prime Directive

I think of our "prime directive" as the guiding foundation of our life. It is a basic assumption we hold about ourselves and the world we inhabit. It informs every decision we make, both consciously and unconsciously. It influences our relationships, our health and our moods.

To the extent that our prime directive is "I'm *not* good enough, loveable or worthy," we are defensive. We worry. We may feel anxious, depressed and hopeless. We may be aggressive and competitive. We could be addicted to behaviors or substances in an effort to conceal the "truth," numb our shame or our emotional pain. We constantly seek validation. We might be acquisitive. We might be a "pleaser" so people will like us or need us.

When our prime directive is "I am exactly, perfectly who I'm supposed to be. I am lovable and worthy," there is nothing to defend. When we are able to make this truth our prime directive, when we replace the negative influence of our Basic Wound with the positive influence of the Truth, we are motivated by our volition, our inspiration, our love and our enthusiasm. We live our life from a platform of inner peace and certainty.

Imagine living your life without questioning your personal value

Imagine living your life, day to day, with a solid sense of well-being. Imagine living your life solving your problems, correcting your mistakes, surviving tragedies and enjoying successes without ever questioning your personal value. How would that change your experience of being human?

RILEY. It took me years to really understand and accept that that my upset, any upset, no matter what it was about, was based in my shame and fear that I'm not lovable or worthy. The realization came as a result of immersing myself first in a meditation practice and later in psychotherapy as a client, a practitioner and teacher.

I learned to acknowledge my shame, understand its roots and how it influenced my life. I learned from experience the relationship between any upset I might feel about a current event and my basic wound from childhood.

If you recall, my early experience convinced me that I was unlovable, unimportant and unworthy. My Coping Strategies included being nice and accommodating so I wouldn't be abandoned; oppositional because I resented the self abandonment that was required in being accommodating; and split off (a space case) to avoid the whole dilemma.

As an adult, I would be upset if I thought I was being excluded. I was hypersensitive to criticism. At one point I would get migraine headaches. I came to realize that they came on when I experienced an inner conflict between being oppositional and accommodating (conflicting coping strategies).

I remember a Saturday morning back in the nineteen-sixties. The phone woke me way too early. My girlfriend at the time was on the line. She was excited. She had a plan for us. It was a beautiful day. She wanted to fix us breakfast, hop in the car, drive to the Angeles Forest to spend a beautiful day hiking.

Long pause. My whole self was silently screaming, "No!"

On the phone, as I came awake, I was beginning to realize that I wasn't feeling well and I was craving a do-nothing day. I was in deep conflict. Out of my conviction that I was not lovable, I was assuming that I had to do what my girl friend wanted to keep her happy or be rejected and lose her. At the same time I resented the hell out of "being put in that dilemma." I was experiencing a self-generated nightmare.

I needed a low energy, do-nothing day. I was afraid to assert my need and was pressuring myself to overrule my desire and resented the pressure.

There was chaos going on inside.

That was a long time ago and I don't remember what we ended up doing that day. What I do remember, vividly, is that the emotional and physical turmoil resulted in a migraine headache.

Eventually I learned to trust that I am lovable and worthy. Now I'm able to say what I want without fear of being abandoned. Now I think of speaking my wants as the beginning of a negotiation between two equal people who care about each other. No more migraines.

BRYAN. My client Bryan, you may recall, connected to his truth, "I am exactly what and who I need to be. From there my doing is guided by inspiration, aspiration, volition and LOVE." So what changed? How did that translate to his daily life?

So far, he has focused more on teaching and mentoring staff within his department at work. Otherwise his work life is the same only with greater success and minimal stress. "There is the story of the Zen master," Bryan says, "The master says to the student that before he was enlightened, he chopped wood and carried water. Now that he is enlightened he chops wood and carries water." Meanwhile Bryan's stomach is calmer, he doesn't yell at his dog and he has reactivated his interest in competitive tennis. His goal is still to win, but his motivation and strategy are altogether different. Instead of striving to overcome his "ineptitude" and be better than his opponent, his new focus is on challenging himself to experience the place of peaceful, focused action. He calls it the timeless zone—and he often wins.

LISA. My client, Lisa, operating from "I'm not good enough," complained of being averse to relationships with men and didn't trust women. Talented, smart and attractive, Lisa felt inadequate, unlovable and ashamed.

Over time, as she embodied her new truth, she more and more allowed herself to feel loved and appreciated. She developed strong friendships, was more assertive in developing her business and ultimately connected with a good life partner.

DAVID. David, as he embraced the certainty that he was "okay," reported being less reactive. He asks for help and makes fewer errors. He said that he felt more even and calm, even when an unexpected difficulty came up.

EVERYTHING CHANGES

So, when you change your prime directive, everything changes–first on the inside and then on the outside. When you base your life on the Lie, you are more or less in constant turmoil. When you base your life on the Deepest Truth about your Self, you are at peace, no matter what is happening around you.

When your prime directive is the truth, "I am perfectly who I am," you are motivated by enthusiasm, love, volition, inspiration and sense of purpose. You have access to compassion—*for yourself and others.* You can think more clearly. You perceive more accurately. You have access to your intuition. You treat yourself well. You are clear that the words and actions of others are not about you, even if they say they are. It's easy to apologize when you mess up and to set things right. As an athlete or a poet, you have access to "the zone." As a musician, you have access to "the groove." As a social or political activist, you are motivated by your inner sense of justice and a strong sense of purpose.

Even when you strive and struggle, you do it in service of your enthusiasm, love, volition,

inspiration and/or sense of purpose. Someone committed to a career in politics might run for office several times before succeeding in being elected. Each failure is seen as a learning opportunity rather than evidence that "I'm not good enough." Ultimately they either succeed at politics or learn that they're not suited for it and go on to find their true calling. Someone with health challenges might alternately persevere and embrace their impediment, never considering themself to be "less than." They heal, or accept their limited ability or die — in peace.

Even when you do boring or odious chores there is no resentment or frustration because you do it in service of your enthusiasm, love, volition, inspiration and/or sense of purpose. When you love an ordered life, for instance, you recognize that it requires a certain amount of effort. So clearing a clogged toilet, doing income tax returns or washing dishes is simply what you do. No big deal.

Even when a tragedy happens you may grieve, you may be shocked, temporarily disoriented, feel disappointed and profoundly inconvenienced, but you won't be upset, shattered, defeated and take it as a sign that you're deficient in some way. You are also open to learning from the experience. Working with trauma victims I notice that people who carry the conviction that they are not good enough or are unlovable are the hardest hit and are more traumatized. The event powerfully triggers their Basic Wound so that they are not only dealing with the shock and loss of the trauma, but they are dealing with "proof positive" that they are not okay. Once they are able to embrace the truth that they are okay they can begin to grieve and to process the shock and loss.

I am not promising nor am I advocating a trouble-free life—far from it. I am suggesting that trouble needn't cause upset, anger or defeat. Trouble becomes simply a problem to solve and/or a lesson to learn. *And that changes everything.*

Maybe it's ordained that being human is a mixed experience. I've come to speculate that our task on Earth is not so much about fixing the world. I've come to believe that our task is to fix ourselves in order to cope with the world and its stresses.

There are mystics who have said that it is part of the Grand Plan that the human experience is a boot camp for the soul's evolution. If that is so, then perhaps "enlightenment" is discovering that place of peace and purpose within while inhabiting and participating in this wonderful and horrendous human experience.[9]

I also choose to believe that the more of us who achieve inner peace and certainty, the less we humans cause trouble for ourselves and each other.

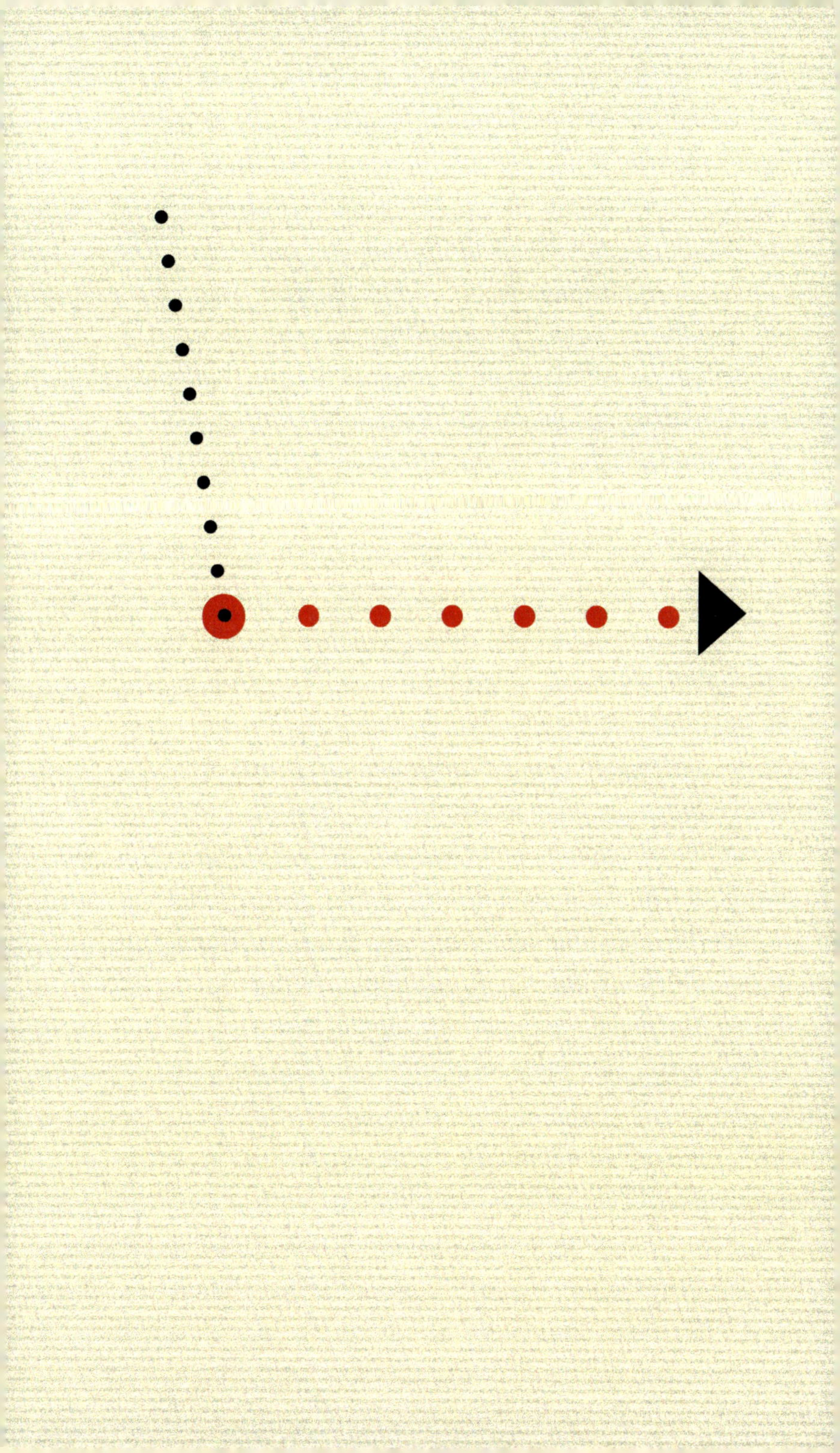

it's

DONe

Appendix

It is not my intention to write a self-help book. However, I have proposed what I believe to be the huge importance of shifting deeply held, psychological prime directives. Actually doing what I've proposed takes a determined effort and I would be remiss if I didn't at least describe some of the tools and processes that I teach my clients and that I've used and continue to use in my own transformation. Perhaps they can be useful to you or inspire you to find your own.

I like to think of the essence of the work as *reprogramming*.

REPROGRAMMING

Here's how I understand it; the complex aspects of the Basic Wound are programmed into the central nervous system, the organs, the muscles, the location and sequence of synapse firing in the brain as well as the emotional reactions and cognitive assumptions about the self and the world. Since the origin of the Basic

Wound is preverbal and/or experiential, the reprogramming has to take place primarily in the body, brain and central nervous system. In other words, our cognitive understanding is our guide, but the change takes place in the body.

> The change takes place in the BODY

There are several new technologies for reprogramming emerging out of our growing knowledge of brain science. Neurofeedback, Eye Movement Desensitization and Reprocessing (EMDR), EFT Tapping, Integrative Body Psychotherapy (IBP), Somatic Experiencing (SE) and Bioenergetics are ones that I know of. I have personal experience with only two of them—IBP and EMDR.

DECIDE

The first step in making a fundamental change such as the reprogramming I'm describing is to make a clear decision to go for it. Having done that, no matter how difficult the process may seem, your will and determination is engaged. You have a goal and a reason to try these inconvenient and, sometimes, preposterous exercises. You have a reason to override the inner resistance that is likely to arise.

MEDITATE

Most of us try to change external circumstances in an effort to feel peace and calm. Ultimately and inevitably that strategy doesn't work. What does work is to feel peace, calm and a solid sense of "I am okay" *regardless* of your circumstances. Then confront your circumstances from that place of clarity, peace and calm. That is my goal when I meditate.

Some people meditate in an effort to split off and mentally get away from upsetting circumstances. That is not the meditation I'm referring to.

By meditation I mean any practice that helps you feel a sense of wellbeing, centered, energized, calm, grounded, and in-the-present. From that place it is easy to know that you are okay and exactly who you are supposed to be.

There are many ways to get to that sense of well-being: chanting, breathing, surfing, swimming, running, yoga, singing, dancing, drumming and walking to name a few. What these activities have in common are breathing, physical motion, and focusing on the present, all without thinking. Walking, running, drumming, dancing and swimming also include bilateral action—alternating right and left motion which seems to have a stimulating and healing influence on the central nervous system.

However, meditating to a state of peace and calm, alive and present is only the first step. For me, there is an important second step to reprogramming. From that meditative state you are receptive to the truth. From that state there is a felt sense of the truth. The truth can be experienced in the body, brain and central nervous system and *that's where the reprogramming takes place*. In that state you are most receptive to your cognitive knowing. That is the time to say and/or write your new truths, in the language of your childhood, "I am worthy, lovable, good, exactly and exquisitely who I am supposed to be." It is important to be conscious of any sensations that occur as you acknowledge and register those truths.

By doing this daily over a period of several months, the truth can become your prime directive.

You may have noticed that in the session dialog with Lisa and David (in Chapter Four), I guided them through that process.

BREATHE

Breathing fully is essential to feeling and being alive. Breathing fully is essential to experiencing a state of well-being. Regulating the breath is also the first and most primal somatic strategy for coping with stress. When an infant experiences the stress of a need not being met, it reduces its breathing to reduce the intensity of the stress it feels. Reduced breathing also makes it impossible to feel fully alive and present. We must breathe fully to experience our Core Self.

reduced breathing makes it impossible to experience the core self

My meditation begins with two breathing techniques I call Charge Breathing[8]. I describe them here. Though it's usually better to have a coach to teach you, feel free to give it a try. There is no downside to trying it.

(It's important to note that Charge Breathing is contra-indicated if you

have epileptic seizures, asthma, panic attacks or are pregnant.)

Charge Breathing I: With jaw and mouth relaxed and open, pull as much air as you can into your upper chest. Then release the air and let it flow out without pushing. Combine this way of breathing with a "cross-crawl" motion. Standing in place, as you inhale, raise your right arm and left leg. As you exhale, lower your arm and leg. On the next breath raise your left arm and right leg. Alternating right and left with each breath, continue this exercise for three to five minutes or until you feel energized, calm, present and grounded.

Charge Breathing II: You can increase the charge with this different technique. Standing with your forearms parallel to the ground and palms pressed together in the center of your chest as if in prayer, with jaw and mouth relaxed and open, pull as much air as you can into your upper chest. This time, however, when you exhale vigorously blow the air out and simultaneously press your palms together. Rapidly repeat this breath 20 to 40 times. This exercise will "pump up" the energy and aliveness very quickly.

Note that it is usually necessary to build a tolerance for aliveness with practice over time. Many people will feel spacy or dizzy when they begin to do these exercises. If this happens, simply stop, get clear and grounded and then continue. When doing Charge Breathing I, the spaciness and dizziness is reduced by focusing on following your hands with your eyes as they go up and down. When doing Charge Breathing II, spaciness and dizziness are reduced by looking around and noticing objects and colors as you breathe.

SELF NURTURE

Having breathed yourself to a sense of well-being, physically, emotionally and mentally, you are fully receptive to acknowledge and embody the truth about your Self. You are amenable to the cognitive reprogramming. At this point say and write your truth, something like, "I am worthy," "I love you," "I am exactly who I am supposed to be," "It's who you are I love, not what you do," or "I am a finite expression of the infinite God." As you say and write your truths, register in your mind that they are true and notice the sensation in your body that accompanies that certainty. The body-mind connection is where the reprogramming takes place.

RESOURCING

"Resourcing" is a meditation tool used in the process of EMDR therapy.[10] You might think of it as self-hypnosis. It seems to help the reprogramming process. Here's a summary of how it works.

There is both clinical and anecdotal evidence that bilateral stimulation (alternate right-left tapping or right-left eye movement) while remembering an upsetting experience deprograms the brain and central nervous system (CNS). It also seems that imagining a positive and calming experience with bilateral stimulation *re*-programs the brain and CNS. This latter phenomenon is used for resourcing.

In your imagination you create 1) a peaceful, safe place, 2) an inner nurturing figure, 3) an inner protective figure and 4) a wise advisor.

One at a time, with bilateral stimulation, you imagine each resource as vividly as possible, acknowledging the sensory experiences that accompany each one—what you see, hear, feel, smell and taste.

As with charge breathing, it's usually better to have a coach to teach you, however there is no harm in trying it for yourself.

WHY PSYCHOTHERAPY IS OFTEN NECESSARY

For most of us, making the change that I'm proposing is difficult or even impossible without help. Why?

The quick answer is that most of us are so convinced that we are fundamentally flawed (Basic Wound) that we never question it. Further, we can be caught in the complex knot of thoughts, beliefs, habits, sensations and emotions of our Coping Strategies and it never occurs to us that there is anything to be done about it.

Most of us will seek help only when we have a crisis: a

life-threatening addiction problem, relationship crisis, panic attacks, clinical depression, suicidal thoughts, or legal trouble, to mention a few.

A good therapist can provide support, safety, insight and understanding, and the mental health tools necessary to sort out the problem, resolve it and move on.

Sometimes the process takes weeks and sometimes it takes years.

Footnotes and Resources

1 Jack Lee Rosenberg with Marjorie L. Rand and Diane Asay, *Body, Self and Soul; Sustaining Integration,* (Humanics Limited, 1985). Rosenberg and Beverly Kitaen-Morse, *The Intimate Couple,* (Turner Publishing, Inc., 1996). https://en.wikipedia.org/wiki/Integrative_body_psychotherapy#References

2 Attachment theory: https://en.wikipedia.org/wiki/Attachment_theory

3 Michael Balint, *The Basic Fault,* (Northwestern University Press, 1992)

4 This treatment process is part of Integrative Body Psychotherapy. (See footnote 1 above and footnotes 5,6,7, and 8 below)

5 Jack Lee Rosenberg and Beverly Kitaen-Morse, *The Intimate Couple,* (Turner Publishing, Inc., 1996), 27.

6 Jack Lee Rosenberg and Beverly Kitaen-Morse, *The Intimate Couple,* (Turner Publishing, Inc., 1996), 215-217.

7 Jack Lee Rosenberg and Beverly Kitaen-Morse, *The Intimate Couple,* (Turner Publishing, Inc., 1996), 43.

8 Jack Lee Rosenberg and Beverly Kitaen-Morse, *The Intimate Couple,* (Turner Publishing, Inc., 1996), 85-116.

9 I want to be clear that I'm not saying that we must passively accept the suffering and injustice in the world. I'm saying that from our place of inner peace we are inspired and motivated to pursue our life's purpose, our true vocation. In doing that we each serve the human race in the way that is the most effective use of our talents. For some that service is in the realm of family and friends. For others that service is on the world stage. For most of us it's somewhere in between.

10 https://en.wikipedia.org/wiki/Eye_movement_desensitization_and_reprocessing

PHOTO CREDIT: MONTY ROWAN

About the Author

Riley K. Smith, MA, is a psychotherapist in private practice in Mar Vista/West Los Angeles. Since 1976, he has worked with adult couples and individuals, helping with anxiety, depression, post-traumatic stress, addictions, relationship problems and adult survivors of childhood sexual and physical abuse.

Mr. Smith teaches his clients mental-health tools, focusing on root causes — usually attachment injuries and the residual effects of early childhood trauma.

As clinical director of an outpatient drug treatment program, he began training therapists in 1996 and in 2002 joined the faculty at the Integrative Body Psychotherapy (IBP) Central Institute in Venice, California. Mr. Smith currently supervises and train therapists at Southern California Counseling Center in Los Angeles.

Mr. Smith is co-author of *How to Be a Couple and Still Be Free,* a problem-solving manual for couples, Fumbled Book Press, 2018 and *TRUE PARTNERS: a workbook for building a lasting intimate relationship,* Tarcher/Perigee, 1993.

He is a member of CAMFT, AAMFT and United States Assoc. of Body Psychotherapists.

Riley K. Smith, MA, LMFT#7928

Mr. Smith posts articles on his website at:
www.rileysbubble.com
Email at: riley@rileysbubble.com

Made in the USA
San Bernardino, CA
18 January 2019